Manage
The Cust

"In today's feature-laden, product-oriented world,
Fitzgerald brings focus and important takeaways about
the real differentiator driving an organization's success:
customer service and its importance to managers and
companies in achieving sustainable competitive
advantage."

Steven Stralser, Ph.D.
Author "*MBA in a Day*"
Clinical Professor,
Walker Center for Global Entrepreneurship,
Thunderbird School of Global Management

"*I have witnessed Fitzgerald's dedication to customer
service for over 20 years and this book contains high
impact lessons managers at every level can learn from.*"

Michael Beach
Former CFO Blackboard, Inc.

"*The Customer First Manager... should be required
reading for anyone in your firm who takes care of a
customer or manages a person who takes care of a
customer, and that is everyone in your firm.*"

Dr. Carl Braunlich
University of Nevada Las Vegas,
Harrah Hotel College

Scully

3/24/12

Special quantity discounts may be available when
purchased in bulk by corporations, organizations
or groups. For information contact
the copyright holder below.

ISBN 10: 1475000154 ISBN 13: 9781475000153

Contents

Introduction

Hello. My name is Mr. Moss and I have spent twenty-five years in Management. Specifically, the Management of Service.

Regardless of whom I was working for or where I was working, I was always managing service. While most companies understand they sell a product and offer a service with that product, I understood early on that service *is* a product. A product that requires as much attention as a recipe, code, display or a product's design if you are to get it right. Over the years, I learned many lessons in addition to this. Lessons that helped me better manage my employees, customers, employers, and myself. These lessons I share with you now because I am leaving the front lines of managing service to work at my company's home office.

To be honest, I am not sure what I will do there. No customers come to the office. Our products are not sold there and few front line employees are there. But before I go, I will leave you with these seven stories. Stories that tell the seven most important lessons I have learned. Lessons that kept my career moving forward, regardless of many other circumstances.

Lesson One from Mr. Moss:

Coach More, Catch Less

Increasing Engagement

Not long ago, while waiting to board a plane home from Chicago, I had one of those exciting moments where a new idea moves you and you know you will never be the same. At the time, we were well-staffed with quality front line Managers who knew how to deliver for the customer. I was a Regional Manager and store sales were up. But something was wrong. Every day was too much of a struggle to get the "to-do" lists done and achieve the profitability we should have been achieving since sales were good. The daily checklists, quality controls and cost controls seemed to be a constant struggle and I could not figure out why.

I reflected on my conversations with the Managers at our location in Chicago. Susan was one of the Assistant Managers I had the opportunity to speak with during my visit.

"How is it going?" I asked.

"Okay," she said. "We are trying to get the staff where they need to be. They still aren't following all of our procedures. I tell them each day at our pre-shift meeting what is expected but it's hard to get people to do what we want, you know? It seems they're not even listening, because right after a pre-shift meeting I catch them doing the things we just asked them not to do and skipping over the things that we want done. "

The conversation continued like this with Susan informing me of all the shortcomings of her staff; how the staff did not do what was asked of them. I then sat down with Matt, the General Manager.

"How is it going?" I asked again.

"Good!" he replied. "But my Managers need to improve their focus. They could be more detail-oriented. I have covered it and covered it in my weekly Managers' meetings but then the next day I seem to be seeing the same mistakes."

He went on to tell me how he seemed to always catch his managers not following procedures or guidelines. He mentioned what a "struggle" it was to get things like cleaning lists, daily walk-thrus and reports completed accurately, while still achieving the weekly goals associated with the budget. Goals like aggressive scheduling and daily labor "cuts" to reduce our labor cost.

I looked out at the planes landing and taking off and all of a sudden it hit me. Our Managers had been focusing on the "catching" and not the "coaching" when it came to managing people.

Instead of getting on a plane home, I went back to the store to sit down with the Management team. Needless to say they were a bit surprised to see me walk back in and call everyone into a meeting on the spot. I asked them all to recap what they had told me about the current state of things. After listening, I asked a question.

"What is the point of a pre-shift meeting with the staff?"

"To communicate to the staff the latest news and expectations," replied Patrick, who was sitting next to Susan.

"Inspect, inform and motivate," added Matt, the General Manager.

"Okay," I said. "But what are your expectations coming out of a pre-shift meeting?"

"For the staff to do what we ask of them in the meeting," Susan said.

"Well, do they?" I asked.

"Obviously not," she said.

"Okay," I agreed. "If it were that easy, I would just video conference in the daily staff meetings." They all laughed as I continued. "Matt, you said 'inspect, inform and motivate' which is great. But of these three points, which one helps manage performance?"

He thought about it and said, "Well, I guess inform sets the expectation for what you want."

"Exactly. A pre-shift meeting is just a place to lay the groundwork for what you will *manage* that day. This is why we have them daily." I added, "How many times do we ask an employee to do something one time and then see it get done by that effort alone?"

"Not often," said Patrick.

Susan added, "And it's so frustrating!"

"Why?" I asked.

"Because they should do what we ask them to do."

"Imagine if they did. What would you do?" I asked.

"Be a lot happier," she replied as they all laughed.

"No really, what would your job be?" I asked. "If all you are is a vehicle to communicate what needs to be done, then with the telephone, fax and internet, I would be a little worried about my job being replaced by technology if I were you."

They all thought about that for a moment.

"Your pre-shift meetings actually have little to do with the problem of getting your staff to do things."

"How would you rate the quality of your employees?" I asked.

"Considering the wages we are able to pay and the labor conditions in this market, I think we're doing well." Matt always knew which questions to answer.

"So the staff is good," I stated and they agreed. "Well then, you need to shift your expectations."

"Why can't we expect them to do what we tell them to do?" Susan asked.

"Well, as I already said, if it were that easy, you wouldn't have a job. Every day I would just video conference in the latest changes and expectations and the employees would do what they were supposed to do without supervision."

"I'd like to see that," said Susan.

"It won't happen," I said with a laugh. Then I got serious. "It won't happen because you are too important. But, you need to change your expectations of how you get things done. Realize a pre-shift meeting lays the groundwork for what you will *manage* that day. You are planting a seed so later in the day you can walk up to an employee and say, 'Good job,' or 'Wait a minute, I thought we agreed we were not going to do this anymore.'"

This sunk in with everyone for a moment, and then I said, "Coach More and Catch Less."

They looked a bit confused so I said it again, "Coach more and catch less. Right now, you all focus on setting the expectation and then catching the results. Change your way of thinking to one where you set the expectation then coach the process through to the end result. In sports, where is the coach during a game?"

"On the sidelines," replied Patrick.

"And what is the coach doing?"

"Helping decide which plays to run and providing immediate feedback to the players."

"Correct," I agreed. "But the point is the coach is engaged in every play. They don't send the team out onto the field with just the playbook. They are a part of the process. They are a part of the *game.* Imagine how your favorite team would do if the head coach sat in the owner's box at the next game."

"So every time an employee needs coaching we should consider it job security?" asked Susan.

"I never thought of that, but yes," I replied. "Your engagement with them and development of them will help ensure their success, which will help ensure the store's success as well as your own. Not to mention it should give you a greater sense of worth."

"How so?" asked Patrick.

"When Susan just asked about job security every time an employee needs coaching, the key word she mentioned was 'need.' You are needed by that employee, which means you are needed by the company. I assume you are all like me and want to feel needed?"

They nodded in agreement.

"I want you all to view each shift this week as a game in your favorite sport. The way you win is by having a pre-shift meeting with your staff to lay out the expectations. Then, as the engaged head coach, you participate in every 'play'- every aspect of the shift that you can, which relates to the topics discussed at the meeting. Regardless of sales that shift, if you did the things that were discussed in the pre-shift meeting, you win. Adopt this attitude of Coach More and Catch Less as your normal operating behavior and I assure you your results will improve. With your involvement, your staff will get the things done you have asked and you'll be much happier."

The meeting adjourned and I asked the General Manager, Matt, to stay behind.

"That was good. Thank you," he said.

"What about you?" I asked. "How will this affect your weekly manager meetings?"

He got it. Matt didn't know it, but he was on the shortlist for a promotion to Regional Manager - my job. I decided to spell it out anyway.

"Matt, I want you to focus on three areas with your managers in your weekly meetings. People, Products and Profits -the three P's. Evaluate your team's performance in these areas during the past week and then set goals for the upcoming week.

Lay the groundwork for your Managers' performance at this meeting, and then be engaged with them every shift with relation to these goals.

Every day, ask your Managers a detailed, pointed question about their responsibilities like, 'how is labor tracking this week' or, 'do you have the product you need for the expected volume this weekend?' Spend time each day in each of your manager's departments, coaching them. I don't care if it's just five minutes, you will see an impact."

"I do rotate through department managers leading the weekly meeting so they stay engaged," he told me. "They all want to run the meeting."

"That's good. They must realize, as I hope you do, that the weekly meeting is just a time to evaluate what has already happened and decide what needs to happen. Nothing really gets done at the meeting. Great ideas can come during a meeting but unless they are implemented, they are just words."

"They need to be coached to the end," he said.

"Correct. Running a meeting is like being a schoolteacher and having to turn in report cards. The grades are set by the quality of the work already done, not the task of formulating the grade. My wife teaches second grade and she taught me that. She believes the students' grades are a reflection of her ability to teach. Shift the importance to the time between the meetings, not the meetings themselves."

"Can I let the Manager with the best performance that week run the meeting?" he asked.

"Now you've really got it!" I exclaimed.

"Can I add a fourth P?" he asked.

"What is it?"

"Positivity."

"I like it," I said. "People, Products, Profits and Positivity."

The next time I was in Chicago, I saw a much happier management team and I already knew by our reporting systems that controls and profitability had improved. Coaching more and catching less worked.

Mr. Moss Advises:

When you *Coach More, Catch Less* your experience, desire, care and education (both formal and street smarts) will make a positive impact and improve the results of all your initiatives. Your staff will learn and grow from your engagement and your supervisor will be impressed with the results when you *Coach More, Catch Less*. This means a different approach than one you may have been using. Rather than verbally communicating the expectations and then being the judge of the outcome, you must communicate the expectations and be involved in many of the steps that lead to the outcome. Like a schoolteacher who grades herself on her students' performance, align your own performance with that of your staff's. Some extra work with a few of your "students" may greatly improve the overall grade.

Use meetings as a chance to plant a seed in each person's brain for the things you plan on managing. Mayor Bloomberg of New York City holds all meetings standing up so people do not get comfortable and start to think of meetings as a time of production.

The message is: *Let's communicate what we need to and go out and get it done.* Tell your staff in meetings you will be following up on the items discussed so they are not surprised when you do.

Remember the four P's of a meeting: **People, Products, Profits** and **Positivity.**

Take pride in your staff needing you to guide them. Don't be frustrated by their needs. Truly recognize these needs as part of your job security. The greater you are able to fulfill the needs of your staff, the greater your job security -as long as those needs are within the acceptable standards of the organization.

"Either love your players or get out of coaching."

-Bobby Dodd, Head Football Coach, Georgia Tech

"The secret to wining is constant, consistent management."

-Tom Landry, Head Coach, Dallas Cowboys

Lesson Two from Mr. Moss:

Throw Strikes

Being the Obvious Choice
for Advancement

I originally went into management with a large retail chain. I was a department manager and was concerned that I was not getting promoted as quickly as others around me.

The Senior Manager at my store, which was the position just below General Manager, had just been promoted and transferred to another location and I wanted the promotion to Senior Manager that she left vacant. I sensed I was not going to get it and thought it was not fair that I remained stuck in this management position while others moved on. Also, if I got a raise and promotion to Senior Manager, I would be one step closer to getting becoming a General Manager.

I approached my General Manager Vickie on the subject and she told me the Regional Manager would be in town and I should sit down and talk with him. Michael, the Regional Manager, sat down with me to discuss this. I pled my case, stating that I worked *so* hard, never called in sick, killed myself for the store and was always on time and willing to stay late.

"I have seen a bunch of managers come through here and get promoted before me. Some even started with the company after I did. And Vickie has it easier than I do. She is the General Manager and people automatically listen to her because of the title. Also, as GM, she makes great money so she has less stress in her outside life and can focus better while she's here because she has less to worry about than I do."

"I see," said Michael.

"So I believe that if I was given the chance to be the Senior Manager in the store, and the salary that comes with this promotion, I would be even more effective."

Michael nodded but was also frowning. He asked me if I played baseball growing up, which I did.

Michael said, "So did I. I even played in the minor leagues for a few years. Can I tell you about it?"

Wondering where this was going I replied, "Sure."

"The monthly minimum pay in the minors is $1,100 plus $20 a day for meals. That's less than $7 per meal each day. We traveled all around the southeast United States in an old bus and stayed at some pretty rough motels."

"Sounds tough," I said.

"It was. Now there are two types of pitchers in the Minors. Both are naturally talented, show up for practice, do what the coaches want and never miss a game. However, one complains about the poor pay and how he is forced to eat fast food, enjoys staying out late with the other team members and having a good time, works hard at practice but does little outside training. The other pitcher makes sure to buy fruits and proteins at the grocery store, gets plenty of sleep each night and even after six hours on a cramped bus will do calisthenics to stay in shape. He is always at practice early and asks the pitching coach to stay late with him. Now this first guy, he doesn't throw that many strikes. When asked why, his response is always the same, 'Give me a big contract and I will give you strikes. Get me off this lousy bus and pay me a million dollars a year and you will see strikes.' The second guy, well, he says no such thing … what do you think happens, Moss?"

"The second guy gets the contract and goes on to the majors."

"Maybe," said Michael. "If he throws strikes, and that's the point. Before you can ask for a promotion, raise or "big contract" you have to throw strikes, period. The first guy wants to blame other things for his inability to throw strikes; the second guy just tries to throw strikes. He does his best, keeps his head down and works every day to throw strikes. If he has the talent, if he throws the strikes, he will get the nod from the boss and move up. If not, he will know he did his best and has no one to blame." He paused for a moment then continued, "And Moss, who do you think the other players and coaches respected? Who do you think *they* were pulling for?"

"Probably the second guy," I guessed.

"Probably," Michael agreed.

I thought for a second then asked, "So are you saying I don't throw strikes?"

"Do you?" asked Michael.

"I already pointed out how hard I work," came my fast reply.

"Your hard work has never been in question. But are you throwing strikes?"

 "I'm always on time."

"Strikes?"

"I worked six days a week the last two weeks and always come in on my day off."

"Strikes, Moss. Strikes."

"I ... I don't know."

He let me compose myself and then asked, "When is your department schedule to be turned in?"

"Tuesday by 10 a.m. for approval by Vickie before being posted on Thursday."

"And when have you been getting yours in?" He asked.

"Tuesday afternoon or Wednesday."

"Why?"

"Well, the weekends are busy and I'm often off on Mondays."

"Ok," he said, "the weekends are busy. Let's talk about that. Are the weekends always busy?"

"Yes."

"So it's no surprise then?"

"No."

"And how many weekends are there in a year?"

"Fifty-two."

"So we have fifty-two weekends a year, every year, and we build these stores to be busy so we can get sales and employ people. Then how can we now use that as an excuse for not getting something done?"

I remained silent.

"How is your ordering?" he asked.

"Okay."

"So you are maintaining the par levels required for your department's volume?"

"I guess I am a little heavy, but I don't want to run out of anything."

"If you maintain the par levels we set forth, you shouldn't. What about that customer complaint you got last month?" he asked.

"I made a mistake and took responsibility for it."

"Of course you took responsibility for it, who else would? But was it a strike?"

After a pause I responded, "I guess not."

"And each day, are you fully prepared for your shift? Is your department checklist complete each and every shift?"

"Vickie does come behind me and check."

"What does she find?"

"She usually can point out a thing or two I may

have missed, but that's her job."

"And that is the point here, isn't it? You want her job, or at least want to get one step closer to it. Moss, setting up for every shift, running every shift, every task and every customer interaction is a pitch. It is you leading your department and you either hit the strike zone or miss. And, just like the big league recruiters, we look at your average. We need to see strikes every day. Way more strikes than not. And when we do, it gets our attention. That makes you the obvious choice and you no longer need to worry about what others are doing or making."

"The obvious choice?" I asked.

"Yes, the obvious choice. When a big league team needs to add a pitcher to their roster, who do you think they look at first?"

"Obviously the one who throws strikes."

"Obviously. So throwing strikes makes you the obvious choice. I should warn you though, sometimes you hit the strike zone and the batter clobbers one out of the park. Those are the big sales days where we move more product than we par up to or that very rare customer who we cannot please. But again, they are rare and if it happens you can still say, 'I threw a strike.'"

I was reflecting on all of my missed strikes in the last few days when Michael asked, "Which type of pitcher do you think I was, Moss?"

I thought about this and replied, "The first, I assume since you are here and not in the big leagues."

"Nope. The second. I was always working hard to throw strikes and taking care of myself. But I didn't have the natural ability so eventually I had to move on." I looked surprise and he saw it.

"Don't be shocked," he said. "I am in the big leagues now. It's just another game, right?"

"True," I stated with the pride I felt for my company.

"And you can be too, Moss. You just need to change your approach to the game and throw more strikes. If you do, your dedication and attitude will make you the obvious choice very soon."

"Throw strikes to be the obvious choice for advancement," I repeated.

"That's it Moss," Michael said simply.

After that meeting, I worked hard to throw strikes every day in every task. I even saw a change in Vickie, too. She soon started using me as an example in meetings as a department manager who could "GM" the department and not need her constant attention.

"When you can be the General Manager of your own department, you are not far from being a General Manager of your own store," she would say.

Mr. Moss Advises:

As a Manager, you must *Throw Strikes* before you will get a raise or promotion. Understand that each customer interaction, each employee engagement and every task you do while working is like a pitch for a professional baseball pitcher. The numbers of things you do correctly are strikes and the mistakes are missed opportunities. Just like a professional baseball team, your employer is keeping track. It is unacceptable to make excuses for missed opportunities. Everyone has challenges, pressures outside of work and distractions. Worrying about what other managers are doing or earning is unprofessional and shows a lack of professional maturity. Very few managers of service are doing a job their supervisor has not done before them and most have people with similar responsibilities at competing locations. This means it is hard to reason your way out of missed opportunities when many before and around you have achieved success in the very same job you have now.

Ask your supervisor what the most important "pitches" are which require strikes every single time. These are the absolute basics that you must do. Recognize that these are the essential tasks that must be done to perhaps even keep your job.

List all of your missed pitches in the last week and your reason for missing them. Then list what you could have done to turn those missed opportunities into strikes. List all of your strikes thrown in the past week. What made them easy and how can you take these results to your missed opportunities? Now set a plan for the coming week to hit the same strikes as last and reduce your missed opportunities.

Keep your own strike average. Understand you will make mistakes. However, talk to your supervisors about your missed opportunities before they talk to you and have a plan to prevent or reduce these missed opportunities. This is a form of self management that is vital to success as a Senior, General, or Unit Manager. When you manage your own location, one very important thing you will have to do is recognize mistakes within the unit and correct them before they affect the customer or the company. The same principle applies to keeping your own strike average and correcting your own behavior.

Recognize the rewards for increasing your strike average. By throwing the most strikes, you will make yourself the obvious choice for advancement or an increase in pay. Employers want people to be successful and need individuals to advance. It is more positive and less costly for the employer to promote people from within the organization. By being the obvious choice, you will actually make your path to promotion easier because you are giving your supervisor an easy decision.

In the restaurant business, you are only as good as your last meal served.

Lesson Three from Mr. Moss:

Smile or You're Fired

Becoming a Customer First Manager

Early in my career I was running a restaurant for a very smart man who was an engineer. We had an excellent chef and terrific food. The owner trusted my judgment and I only called him when absolutely necessary. I was confident in both my, as well as our assistant manager Brian's, abilities. We managed the standards the owner set forth and ran a very tight ship. We received excellent health inspections, maintained a beautiful facility and hit the cost controls as dictated by the owner.

However, it came to my attention that we were receiving far too many customer complaints via email. This confused me since I felt we had a tight grip on the operation. So I decided to call the owner and ask him for his help. He was already aware of our dedication and focus and how we would "write-up" staff for any violations. He asked me if this was something we were consistent with and I assured him it was. He instructed me to gather all of our recent employee disciplinary write-ups and customer complaints. He wanted me to review them and look for parallels. "Connect the dots," he said.

I decided to engage Brian in the process. So one afternoon we sat down at a table and organized two piles. One had all of the employee write-ups, and the other, all of the customer complaints. I decided to read aloud the first customer complaint, then Brian would read aloud the first employee write-up and we would compare. The first complaint I read was about a hostess not being very accommodating on the telephone when a customer had called to make a reservation. The customer understood we were full at the time she wanted to come in but did not appreciate the tone that our hostess used while denying her the chance to come in when she wanted. Then Brian read an employee write-up that concerned an employee who was ten minutes late.

Honestly, I sat there wondering what to do next and Brian, with his black and white mentality, said, "Let's write one word to describe each customer complaint and write-up and compare the two at the end."

Ok, I thought but added, "Let's reread each and look for something beyond the written word."

Brian raised his eyebrows but did not object. I read mine again and said, "What's interesting to me is that the customer never even had the chance to eat here yet was still dissatisfied. I am sure she went somewhere else for dinner so we got the complaint but not the sale. The word here is 'tone.'"

Brian raised his eyebrows again, reread his employee write up, looked up and said, "Nothing interesting. Employees need to be on time."

So I asked what time was the employee scheduled and he said three pm. Interesting to me, I noted, we don't open until five in the evening. Brian shrugged his shoulders and said the word here was 'tardiness.'

The next complaint came from a couple who had come in for their anniversary, purchased a bottle of wine, yet did not feel that our staff had any interest in making the occasion special. Next, Brian read of an employee who had on the wrong color socks. The word I chose was 'needs.' Brian wrote 'uniforms.'

The next complaint was from a customer who was

not happy that his wife and daughter had been referred to as "guys" by our staff. As in, "How are you guys doing?" The complaint was titled, "My Wife is Not a Guy." Brian then read of an employee who failed to properly organize the storage room at the end of a shift and wrote down 'side-work' while I wrote down 'language.'

We continued on and here is what our list looked like:

Brian's (Write-Ups)	Mr. Moss's (Complaints)
Tardiness	Tone
Uniforms	Needs
Side-work	Language
Shaving	Friendliness
Theft	Urgency

As we just began to review the list, one of our top servers, Kate, entered the room. Kate was great. She was respected by staff and management. She had many regular customers who loved her. I explained what we were doing, and with the staff write-ups safely out of sight, I asked her to review the list and give us her thoughts. I told her we were looking for parallels. She read the list and said with a smile, "There are none."

Wow, I thought. Are we this out of touch with our customers' needs? "We have got to figure out how to manage the items on my list of complaints." I continued, "We cannot be this out of touch with our customers' needs and expect to succeed."

Just then Brian interrupted my thought with, "We do a great job running this place, you can't please everybody. I mean, what are we suppose to do? *Not* manage our employees to make sure they are on time and properly dressed, not stock up so we are ready and turn a blind eye to theft?" There was silence for a minute.

"Why can't we do both?" Kate said.

I noticed two things about her comment. First, it was more of a sentence than a question. Second, she said "We." Boy, she did care.

"But how?" asked Brian.

"Figure out what the customer wants and manage it first," said Kate.

"Exactly," I encouraged. "You are exactly right, Kate. We need to take our same ability to manage the checklists of the business to also manage the needs of the customer. Let's discuss what the customer wants."

Brian asked how and I suggested we use the list of complaints as a guide. We reviewed the list of guest complaints and I asked Brian if there were any patterns, to which he impressively answered, "Attitude."

"Okay, let's manage it," I said.

He replied, "You can't. People either have a good attitude or they don't."

Kate, who had been listening intently, chimed in. "But you *can* manage the perception of attitude to the customer." We both looked at her as she went on. "Do you all think I'm really this happy every day? I know that if I put on a smile I'll get one in return. And I like it when someone smiles at me. So no matter what's going on, I put on a smile."

"But not everyone is like you," said Brian.

"True," she said with that smile, "and not everyone has to be, except when they are with the customer."

Once again Kate hit the nail on the head.

I said, "That's it Brian. We create a list of acceptable behaviors with regard to interacting with the customer." Brian leaned forward as I went on. "Just like we have approved behavior for everything from when to show up to where to store the supplies, we will create and have approved behavior for interacting with the customer."

Brian, still leaning forward but ever the skeptic, asked, "Like what?"

I got it, but wanted Brian to get it on his own so I asked him what tools do the employees use with the customers.

"Tools?" asked Brian.

"Yes, tools. A schedule is just a tool for you to let people know when to be here, a uniform guide is a tool to let people know what to wear. So, again, I ask you what are the tools our employees use with the customers?"

Brian looked at Kate and said almost as a question, "A smile?"

"What else?" I pressed.

"Uh, a compliment?" he mustered.

"A compliment is great but it is the words, right? The language."

Kate jumped in, "I have never understood why customers say 'thank you' to us. I know it is just good manners. But really, we should be thanking them. I mean, how many choices do they have for restaurants? 'Have a good day' and 'have a good night' are nice, but a sincere thank you is much more important. When I buy anything I always look for a thank you at the end of the transaction more than anything, and as a server I make sure to get the customer's attention and give them a sincere 'thank you' every time."

Brian started to nod as this sunk in. Knowing he would get this, I asked him about the word 'urgency' on our list and he opened up.

"When a customer asks for something, get it directly, just like the game Monopoly, do not pass go."

"Pass go?" asked Kate.

"Yes," Brian responded. "Do not stop to chat or look at your schedule while in the middle of a task for the customer. Have a sense of urgency to show the customer their needs come first."

I decided to take the lead. "Okay, we will make a list of acceptable words, the language our people can use with customers."

"What you're really doing is creating a list of words we can't use," stated Kate.

"True." I noted. "It will have to be both."

"I can manage a list," said Brian.

We role played as many interactions between customers and employees as we could think of and came up with a list of words we felt represented our brand.

We substituted 'no problem' with phrases like 'my pleasure' or 'absolutely.' Based on the complaint we had read, we decided to ban the phrase 'you guys' from the building altogether. Even two 'guys' were to be called 'gentlemen.' We thought of all the different needs our customers had. Some were in a hurry to catch a movie; others wanted to make a night of it; some wanted to talk; others just wanted service. Our needs list included things like asking parents if children wanted their food first to keep them occupied. We committed to keep a movie listing at the bar and I told the chef we would have to be more flexible on making changes to menu items. After we had made the list, Brian announced, "We're done."

"Actually Brian," I said, "we've only just begun. This was the easy part, now we have to communicate these lists to the staff and ensure they get on board."

Brian wondered aloud how we would communicate this and Kate once again came to the rescue. "Put this in writing and have everyone sign it," she said.

Brian seemed satisfied and once again announced our completed victory.

"That's a good first step, Kate." Brian looked at me as I continued. "But the hard part is managing it. Managing what the customer wants first will be a daily challenge and reminder. Even with the signed document, many employees will not fully understand this, so our management focus must widen. Every day we will have to coach and train this."

Brian asked how. "Kate?" I asked. "What happens when you're late?" She replied as we expected that she would be in trouble. I asked her why that was.

"Because every day Brian or you monitor in times and who shows up when."

I looked at Brian and asked, "Now what will we do?"

"Monitor the things the customer cares about most."

"Every day," I said.

"But it's not always possible to manage everything," said Brian in a rare sign of vulnerability. "I mean, as much as we try, this place is not perfect."

I commended him on a good point and asked Kate

what we should do. "You guys, I mean gentlemen, are great. You get so much done I truly believe you can do this and not let the 'inmates run the asylum' but you have to manage the things the customers want first."

The compliment worked with Brian and he sat straight up and announced, "Customer First Management, that's what we will call it!" He liked a name for everything and there it was. Best of all, he had named it.

"Correct, Brian. We will manage the things that matter to the customer most with the most detail. Customers don't care if someone is five minutes late when we are not even open," I said.

"Do they really care whether we have black or blue socks on?" asked Kate.

"No, and they don't even care if someone steals because we aren't properly locking our safe," I responded.

"They really just want a smile," commented Kate.

"So it's Smile or You're Fired," said Brian.

"*What?*" Kate and I said together.

He continued, "Really, if we are going to be Customer First Managers, then we need to manage the things the customer cares about with the most conviction. Think about it, we can explain almost any mistake we make, and we make them every day. We can explain a mistake with an order, or the kitchen taking too long because we are busy or being behind at the front door. It costs us because we usually have to buy the customer something when we make those mistakes. But the customer understands mistakes happen and accepts our response. That is why we're not getting emails about these types of issues. We manage these things and can fix them with the customers."

It was Kate's turn to get it. "But you cannot explain or buy your way out of an attitude problem, can you?"

"That's right," replied Brian. "The customer won't listen and since we have not been managing those things, the customer leaves unhappy. Some have written in, many have not, but the point is that we need to adopt the same attitude our customer has. In some areas they are patient and understanding and others they are not."

"Smile or You're Fired," Kate pondered. "I like it. It certainly is clear." This made us all laugh. "Imagine if the managers always smiled?" she said in another question-statement.

I looked at Brian and he looked at me and we knew what we had to do. Lead by example just like we did by being on time ourselves.

So we did it. We made a list of acceptable language and behavior for almost every guest interaction. We made smiling at the customer mandatory. We signed it ourselves and had all of the employees sign it and every day at our staff pre-shift meetings, we included points from it in addition to our normal routine of product education and policy reminders. Kate was great, as expected. She worked to do the things the customer wanted first and would give me a wink every time I caught her doing something right and I would point it out in front of the rest of the staff.

More importantly, we truly became Customer First Managers. Each shift we monitored our staff's customer interactions and coached and learned with them what Customer First Management required. We led by example and used the language we demanded for our customers with our employees.

Mr. Moss Advises:

The point of this story is not to allow theft, tardiness or other violations of company rules, just as long as the employee is providing good customer service. Do not let the inmates run the asylum. The point is to manage the things that affect the customer with the same conviction you manage things like stealing and being on time. By lining up your management priorities with your customers' needs, you will become a customer first manager and greatly improve your own, and your organization's chance of success.

Also, understand that customer interaction (also called touch points) can be trained and demanded. In a high-end steak house, a cook is taught to prepare a thick steak to a Medium Rare temperature and to do it hundreds of times per night. This requires focus and conscious actions from the cook. If a cook can be trained to do this over and over again, can a food server be trained to consciously smile at all customers? Can a server be trained to never use the phrase, "no problem" with a customer? The answer is yes. It just requires a desire and focus of managers to make it happen.

Ensure your management priorities are in line with your customers' needs by having a frank discussion with your supervisor about what your management priorities are and what the priorities of the customers are. Connect the dots.

Communicate with your staff what the priorities are with regard to customer service. If possible, update training manuals to have these items covered at the outset of training to highlight their importance. Provide them with clear instructions on what is acceptable and what is not with regard to every point of customer interaction. Provide a list of forbidden words that are never to be used with customers. Include a list of positive alternatives to the forbidden words.

Find a 'Kate' or two whom you can enlist to help you become a Customer First operation or department. Praise them for positive customer interactions in front of the staff with comments like, "Kate, your smile made that customer's day."

Ensure you and your staff always say, "Thank you" to your customers; it means so much more than "Have a nice day." A thank you recognizes your customer's effort in the transaction.

"A smile is nature's best antidote for discouragement.
It brings rest to the weary,
Sunshine to those who are frowning,
And hope to those who are hopeless and defeated.
A smile is so valuable that it can't be bought,
Begged, borrowed, or taken away against your will.
You have to be willing to give a smile away
Before it can do anyone else any good.
So if someone is too tired or grumpy to flash you a smile,
Let him have one of yours anyway.
Nobody needs a smile as much
As the person who has none to give."

-Dale Carnegie
Author of *How to Win Friends and Influence People*

Lesson Four from Mr. Moss:

You Can Never Be Too Fair

Finding Balance as a Manager

Once I began throwing strikes back in my department store days, I was promoted. The combination of my dedication, and my increased focus on results, made me the obvious choice. An opening occurred (as they always do) and Vickie, the General Manager, had no choice but to promote me to Senior Manager. Michael, our Regional Manager, signed off because Vickie had been singing my praises for months.

Things seemed to be going well but I was definitely carrying a large amount of stress with the new responsibility. Now, the reach of my responsibility was far greater. Rather than just being responsible for my team of hourly employees in my department, I was responsible for other managers and *their* employees. It seemed that whenever a problem happened, I was on the other side of the store, or even off that day, but I was still responsible. I was trying to have fun and keep the workplace positive while working to maintain company standards. The constant pressure, however, was getting to me.

"If you permit it, you promote it." This is what Michael told me the day I got promoted.

So I was working hard to enforce standards and prevent problems from occurring.

Kelly had taken the Manager position of my previous department. This was a lateral move for Kelly who came from another store where she had been a Department Manager. After a few months I noticed many of my problems were coming from my old department.

One day while walking through my old department I saw some of our employees chatting and laughing loudly. I looked around and noticed the area was a little messy and two customers who were not even being acknowledged, much less helped.

As I approached, I realized Kelly was in the group.

"What's going on?" I asked.

"Kelly was telling us about her weekend," Ed replied.

I was enraged. "This is unacceptable. We have customers nearby, this area is a mess and you all are chatting? Break it up and get to work!" I turned and stormed off. As I walked away I noticed one of the customers give me a strange look and her husband mumbled, "Lighten up Francis."

The next day I ran into Ed, who had been in the group the prior day, and he asked me what my problem was. Why had I snapped at them? I told him my concern about the lack of focus and he replied that Kelly made work much more fun than I had. She knew how to loosen up. Ed had worked for me when I ran that department and we never had issues like the one I was seeing now.

I knew Kelly was off so I headed for her department to do some digging. Again, when I arrived, I did not find things as they should be and confronted the crew.

"Here we go again," I said to the staff. "The cat is away and the mice are playing."

"What?" a few asked.

"Don't get smart," I said and began to list their shortcomings. I knew one had been three minutes late that day, another was wearing a brown belt instead of a black belt as required and two had forgotten their name tags.

After letting them have it for a minute, I gave them clear instructions on getting the department ready to open, which was in ten minutes.

From that point on I spent a lot of time in my old department and began really cracking down on all departments. Every time I walked through an area I found at least three things wrong and would let the staff know. I was a stickler for punctuality and checklists. I was not about to have performance suffer under my watch. Kelly ended up being my biggest challenge. It was hard and I could not do it every day. Some days I would just ignore the issues for fear of blowing up in front of a customer again.

Kelly believed in being supportive, humanistic and democratic. She was also a big believer in "no harm no foul" and would say if we take care of our people, they will take care of the customer.

One day while Vickie was on vacation, Michael, the Regional Manager, came into town. He asked if he could sit down with Kelly and me. I could not wait. I knew where this was going. He would need me to be a witness to Kelly's poor performance and destruction of my former area of responsibility. I was sure he would use me as an example of success since I had just been promoted.

"We have a problem," he started, "or as they say today, an opportunity."

Here it comes, I thought.

"Moss, your performance is of concern and I want to have a healthy discussion with you about it. I believe Kelly will be of value and have asked her to be here."

What?

"Moss, since becoming a Senior Manager you have become extremely direct with your people. You fail to engage in any form of communication that is not a direct order from you."

I cut him off. "How have my results been?"

"We will get to that in a minute. Kelly, how would you describe Moss here as a supervisor? What has your staff been saying as of late?"

She paused a moment then said, "Tough." She obviously was not exactly comfortable with this discussion in front of me.

"Go on," Michael encouraged.

"Um … profit minded, autocratic, hard-nosed, a drill sergeant. A person who only sees the results and not the people who make the results happen."

"That's it?" Michael asked.

"Well, he is not much fun, that's for sure."

"So the staff is not overly thrilled with him?"

"Ah, no. He needs to lighten up."

"Okay, thank you Kelly. A minute ago I said we have an opportunity here and you could help. Now, Mr. Moss, please describe Kelly to me."

Being shocked at this attack, I stumbled for a minute since this was not the next question I expected. I was still trying to digest her comments about me.

"Um. Okay. I find Kelly a little loose. She is more of a buddy than a boss. She puts the employees before the customers. Her department is not always ready to open on time and there has been more than one complaint recently from customers who had been in her department."

Michael sighed and let the recent comments hang in the air a minute.

"What does her staff think of her?" he asked me.

"They love her because she lets them do whatever they want."

Another minute of silence passed.

"Here is how I see it. Follow me on this one. Kelly's employees are happy with her, but her supervisor and potentially the customers are not happy about her results." He then looked at me. "Kelly and her staff, your employees, are not happy with you but the customers and me pretty much are … now do you know why I am here?"

Nobody said anything.

"Moss, you do need to lighten up. I am not saying lighten up on our standards and guidelines. I am saying lighten up on our people. And Kelly, you need to toughen up. Again, I do not want to take away the loyalty and morale you have created among your staff, but you need to ask yourself at what price are you gaining these things."

We both leaned in to listen as Michael went on.

"You can never be too fair. You can be too nice and you can be too tough, but you can never be too fair."

We needed more and Michael knew it.

"In my career I have often heard people say of a former boss, 'I can't work for that guy, I love him but he's too nice and I was always making up for everyone's slack.' And I've heard, 'I can't work for her, she's too tough on people.' But I've never heard anyone say, 'I can't work for him, he's too fair.'"

"Moss, take a page out of Kelly's book and find some balance in your communication. Smile and chat with people for a second before giving a directive. While I'm happy with the results you have achieved thus far, I know they can't last. Your people will tire of you and turnover will kick in. Morale will soon drop, too. For everything you correct, find something to compliment. When you do direct, take the time to explain why the thing you are asking for is important and the positive result it will create for the customer or company. I would guess you are already managing harder some days than others because you've exhausted yourself by mid-week."

How did he know that?

"And Kelly, you need to recognize that laughs are great but not at the expense of the customer or company's objectives. Have fun with the standards, keep things lively but do it while in a state of productivity. While I always learn when I listen to staff, this is not a democracy. It is a for-profit business and unless we are productive and take care of the customers, we will not have the sales or money to keep people employed. How fun would that be? Also, how nice is it to be having fun with the staff but ignoring the customers? How do you think the customers feel when they have to interrupt a personal conversation to get help? The competition for our product is too steep. We can't make customers feel as if they are an intrusion on our good times. You both need to use the sandwich method when communicating with your staff."

Kelly asked what that was as I remembered the phrase, which I had not heard in some time.

"Think of every directive as a sandwich with three parts: the bottom piece of bread, the meat and the top piece of bread. The meat in the middle is the directive but it must be surrounded by two positive comments on either side, which is the bread. So if I want to ask an employee to straighten up an area, which would be the meat of the conversation, I need to find two positive things to say as well. Here's an example: 'Hi Ed, thanks for being on time today, can you straighten this table before we open? Thank you. Oh, and nice job on that secret shopper last week.' You see, it's a sandwich. Kelly, you need to add meat and Moss here needs way more bread."

Michael continued. "Consistency is another aspect of trying to be fair. Moss, you have been consistent but are burning out from the negativity. Manage a few less things per day but add the bread and you'll feel much less tired at the end of the day. Also, your people will respond better and want to do these things for you -like when you were a Department Manager. Then you won't be finding the same problems over and over again. Kelly, you need to sit down with Moss and write down five things he wants to see better results on. Then make those things the meat in your conversations."

We both left the table with a little more respect for each other. I began going into Kelly's department with a couple nice big pieces of bread to talk about and she made a point of putting some meat into her staff conversations when I was around. We both grew.

Mr. Moss Advises:

Striving for fairness is to be a daily goal for all Managers. Be consistent and always look for positive things and areas that need improvement at the same time. Then address them both at the same time. Another thing I believe in is to never stop giving feedback. The reality is that most people do most things well. If you are providing feedback constantly, then you are likely to be providing a fair amount of praise. If you only speak when something is wrong, then all your employees ever hear is something negative from you. If you are always seeing and commenting on the good things, no matter how small, when you comment on something wrong, it is no big deal. Think of your communication like the ocean's waves at the beach- constant waves delivering a certain amount of water on the shore. Your feedback should be like this throughout the day- consistently delivering what you see, both good and bad. Not saying anything but the few mistakes that may happen each day is like hitting the beach with a tidal wave. It is shocking to your staff.

Consistency breeds trust, which is the pulse of any relationship.

Lesson Five from Mr. Moss:

Know the Numbers

Impacting Profit as a
Customer Service Manager

Profit is often communicated out as "not the goal, but the outcome." While the latter half is true, I want to be honest about the first part. Profit creates many, many things that benefit managers, employees, and customers. Think about this: when profits are down, one of the first things cut are benefits to managers and their employees.

Patrick, the Manager who had learned to *Coach More, Catch Less* was coming up quickly. He had really improved his ability to lead and motivate and was focused on moving his career forward. He was in charge of a labor department in one of our units. This department represented about four percent of our costs. We were in the midst of a growth period so in addition to acting as a Regional Manager, I was on our expansion committee that approved locations and met with banks to help finance our growth. One of the key aspects the banks were looking for was a sense of security that we could repeat our financial performance in a new unit, which would have a loan against it. In other words, could we be as profitable at future units, which they were loaning us money to build, as we are at our existing units?

During a meeting, the banker pointed out that Patrick's unit was not maintaining the same costs as our other units. A couple departments' costs, including Patrick's, were above the average of all our other locations and the bank was concerned this may be a new trend. Assuring the bank that this was "an occurrence and not a trend," I headed straight to Chicago after the meeting.

Matt, Patrick's General Manager, and I sat down. Matt told me how Patrick was very much worried about customer experience and being engaged in leading his employees. However, he couldn't understand why it was not okay to have a little overtime and expand our labor hours given the location's revenue. We called him in to join us.

"Hello, Patrick," I said. "Matt tells me great things about your leadership and dedication to customer service."

"Great. Thanks Matt," Patrick replied.

"But we need something. We need you to raise your performance in another area. Raise it like you have as a leader."

"Okay, I love a new challenge." Patrick was excited.

"Well, it's not a new challenge. It's a challenge you just haven't overcome yet. The challenge is hitting the budget. The shortfall on profitability in this location has caught the attention of the higher ups and the banks that finance us. Tell me about the challenges you have been having in this area."

Patrick thought about how hard he wanted to push this and surprisingly went for it.

"You know, I see the numbers and I know how profitable this unit is. I really don't see how a few dollars here or a percentage there can make that big of a difference. The way our week works, we are often managing overtime during some busy periods. We won't close the door because I miss my budget by a percent or two."

"You think not?" I asked.

"No. The relatively few dollars spent, which reduce profitability a little, go towards the customer and really make things better around here. More than once I have wanted to say, 'just take the overtime cost out of my paycheck,' to make the point of how much I care."

We all thought about that for a minute.

"Patrick," I said, "I understand your perspective. You don't see how your managing tight costs affects the bigger picture. It's not clear to you like coaching more and catching less."

"That's right," Patrick replied.

"You are looking at this in a vacuum."

"Excuse me?" Patrick asked.

"A vacuum. You only see this one piece, but your contribution here has a huge effect on many, many things. Also, just like you must manage your people consistently, all of us including you must manage our costs in the same way. Let me explain. What is our profit as a percentage of sales here?"

"Twelve to fifteen percent, depending on the time of year," Matt answered.

"Alright. So Patrick's budget is roughly four percent of sales, correct?"

"Yes."

"Well, missing your budget by one percent is not really one percent, it is twenty five percent. One is twenty five percent of four. Get it."

Patrick said, "Yeah, but ..."

I cut him off. "But if every manager missed their budget by twenty five percent, then what would our profit be?"

Patrick could not grasp it.

"Nothing." I said. "We just stated our current profit is fifteen percent. If we increased all of our costs by twenty five percent, then our fifteen percent profit turns into a ten percent loss."

Patrick was catching on but I could still see he did not grasp the whole picture.

"Also, Patrick, if you cannot manage this department within budget, why should I believe you can manage your own unit as a General Manager? If Matt missed his budget by twenty five percent he would likely lose his job. You showing you can manage this budget gives us the confidence to increase your budgetary responsibility which translates to raises and promotions."

That got his attention.

"So Patrick, just like you must manage every employee as fairly as possible, so must I. If you're to continue your career forward, as you have, you must understand that you are competing against other managers here. But, let's set that aside for a minute. Let me ask you a question. How does profitability affect the employees and customers?"

"I guess it keeps us from going out of business."

"True," I said. "But let's be more optimistic. This company started with one location. How is it you got your job and position?"

"The company grew and needed managers, I guess."

"That's right. And the only way a company can grow is if it is profitable. No bank will lend a company money to grow unless they see a history of profit, which helps to ensure loans will be repaid. Patrick, do you want to be a General Manager some day?"

"Of course."

"And there are others out there who want your job now. Well, there are two ways to make that happen. Grow, so more positions become available, or wait for turnover among the managers to create an opening. Either way, profitability is part of the equation. We are profitable and grow, or you show you can manage profitability and get the promotion because we believe you'll make us more profitable."

"But how does profit affect the employees and customers?" Patrick asked.

"What happens when a company becomes less profitable is that the company starts to make cuts to costs. This means your labor budget will only get smaller the less profitable you are. So the employees' hours will get cut and they will earn less money for their families and themselves. Fewer employee hours means fewer workers helping customers. It is like a bad snowball. Other costs that could be cut include insurance and sick leave. Profits are part of the equation in order to survive and thrive. Many companies seem to survive despite the poor product they sell. Many may survive despite poor, or zero, service. But there's not a company on the planet that can survive without profit. Hitting your budget is important to all of these things. Do you understand?"

"I do now," Patrick said. "And I assure you I will hit our budgets so we can get our employees their hours and benefits, take care of the customer, and expand."

Mr. Moss Advises

Understand each piece of the profit is important. It contributes greatly to the overall future of your career and your employees. Sit down with your supervisor and ask him or her to explain to you each line in the profit statement. Ask questions about the greater impact of each area and what the average cost is for the whole company for each area. While your commitment to profit must be more subtle than your commitment to customer service, it cannot be a lesser commitment. Profitability is the driving force behind security and growth in business.

"I have made the tough decisions, always with an eye toward the bottom line."

- Donald Trump

Lesson Six from Mr. Moss:

Nobody Ever Said,
"I want to be a cashier when I grow up."

Understanding the
Front Line Employee

Remember Susan from Chicago who learned to *Coach More, Catch Less*? Well, about three months after that meeting she called me. She was feeling much better about her role and the results she was getting. But she was very frustrated with the fact that she *had* to be so engaged.

"When I was an hourly employee, I did what my boss asked me to do," she told me. "I understand Coach More and Catch Less and have seen the results. But I still find it bothersome that if I am not fully engaged in the process, things won't go as well. It's like, if I don't do it myself, or at least stay on top of it, it won't get done right. I remember doing the job my employees do and I worked to make my boss's life easier."

I flew to Chicago to see her and discuss her concerns. She had been with the company eight years; five as an hourly employee and three as a manager. Before that, she was with one of our competitors for four years so she had about a dozen years in the industry.

When I arrived, she told me she had spoken to Patrick about her call to me. She asked if Patrick could sit in on our conversation since he was feeling as frustrated as she was. I agreed. In the fourteen months that Patrick had been with us, he had gained a lot of professional maturity- learning to *Coach More, Catch Less* as well as committing to *Know the Numbers* to impact profitability. Still, this was Patrick's first "real job" since graduating from college and he was motivated to get his career going. We sat down, and after Susan repeated what she told me on the telephone, I asked her, "Why do you think when you were an employee it was different?"

"Well, I did exactly what was asked of me and even made suggestions on how to improve things around here."

"That's good," I said. "But *why* are your employees not behaving the way you did?"

"Because they don't care, I guess."

"Really?" I asked. "So, John over there, who's been with us, what, four years, he doesn't care about this place?"

"Well, he cares."

"Like you did?"

"Kind of …"

"So maybe we should put him into management so he can follow your path."

"He doesn't want to go into management. He likes the flexible hours he has now, being able to get a shift covered on short notice, and the time with his family. He and his son go camping almost every weekend."

"Fair enough," I allowed. "What about Kim? She has been here about a year, does she care?"

"Yes, but her priority is her schooling," Patrick replied. "She is finishing a degree in music and that is her primary focus."

"Okay, so they care but just are not making what we want a priority?"

They nodded in agreement. "How about Megan? What's her story?"

Susan replied, "She needs to go. That one does not care and if we aren't on her, she will cut a corner."

"So why is she even here?" I asked.

"She has mouths to feed," Susan said.

I decided to switch directions and said, "Let's talk about how each of you got here. Susan, you go first. Tell me how you got to this point in your career."

She told me about her work history and how she decided she wanted to take her pride to the next level and go into management. She was at a point in her life where she felt it was time to move beyond a 'job' and start a career. Rather than go back to school, which really was not an option anyway, she decided to use her years of experience to walk into a good paying Management position with us. The benefits were good and the opportunity for growth and advancement had been attractive.

"How about you, Patrick?" I asked.

Patrick told me of his desire for a long career in this business. He wanted my job someday. He had excelled at the State College, working weekends and keeping a full load so he could graduate in four years. Now he had a pile of student loans which needed to be repaid and was anxious to get ahead.

I let these stories set in for a minute then asked, "So both of you are fairly happy with where you are, career-wise, given the choices you had and the decisions you have made?"

They agreed.

"What about John?" I asked.

"What about him?" asked Patrick.

"Is he where he wants to be, career-wise, I mean?"

Susan said, "He told me how he had to drop out of school when his wife got pregnant."

"Really?" asked Patrick.

"So he ran out of choices real fast," I thought aloud.

Patrick was getting it. "And Kim's priority is school so this is just a means to an end. I've been there. While I was in school, I worked at a restaurant bussing tables. The job gave me the hours that worked best with my schooling. I had fun with the people I worked with, but man I hated that job."

Susan was looking at Megan who had just returned to her cash register from the break room.

"She is always calling her family," Susan said. "In the break room she is always on the phone with her kids who are being watched by their aunt."

"She must worry about them," I said.

"Patrick, you are where you want to be. You made a choice to be in this business early on and are working to conquer it. Susan, you made a decision later in life to be here. And while you likely had fewer choices than young Patrick here, you still made the best choice you could and are working to capitalize on it. Remember, nobody ever said I want to be a cashier when I grow up. Actually, few said I want to be a Manager when I grow up but here we all are, together."

"I wanted to be a Fireman when I was a kid," Patrick said. "But something changed and this career seemed like a better fit."

"I wanted to be a nurse but the schooling was not an option so I just started working, enjoyed what I was doing and decided to make the most of it," Susan added.

"It has been said that this is a transient business. People come and go like a bus stop. But I think of our role in these people's lives as that of one like a port for a ship. When a ship comes into port it takes what it needs from its time there. This may be food, water, fuel or rest for the crew. But when it is time to move, the ship unties from the dock and sails away. Many of our most important people are the same as those ships. We are not their destination; we are a port along the journey. Maybe that journey is to a music career for Kim, or maybe it's a journey of survival for Megan. And maybe things will change in John's life when his son is older and he will begin his career-journey here with us and go into Management. Either way, they are getting what they need and we need to understand that there is only so much they are going to give."

"So don't expect them to care?" asked Susan.

"No," I replied. "I am not saying that. Ships do not use a port without a fee. They have to buy fuel and food. So they too must understand that this relationship must be mutually beneficial. So asking them to follow our standards is the 'fee' we ask in return for a paycheck and benefits to help them along their journey. However, just asking won't work."

"Yes, we know, Coach More and Catch Less," said Patrick.

"Correct. And by doing so, by being engaged, you will inevitably find people who are not willing to pay that fee. Ultimately, not everyone will be welcome in our port because they just will not follow the standards we set forth and some even work to upset the dock. But many, like the people we talked about here will get the job done with the proper coaching. We just can't expect them to care like we do. Imagine if everyone in the world wanted to do what we do."

"It would be a pretty boring place," Susan said, which made us all laugh.

"It would, I agree. It takes all types of people and interests to make the world interesting. Besides, if everyone wanted to be in Management like us, there may be some pretty stiff competition." They laughed as I continued. "But really, there's nothing wrong with having a conversation with a Kim or a John and letting them know that you understand and respect their priorities but in the three to six hours a day, four or five days a week they are here, they need to make our priorities theirs. Then they can spend the rest of their time pursuing their music or whatever they wish and we are glad to support that journey."

I followed up with Susan and Patrick a few weeks later. Both said that, even though our conversation did not change the need for them to stay fully engaged, they definitely felt less frustrated about the environment and found themselves a little more understanding of their employees. They were surprised to find that this actually made their employees try harder.

Mr. Moss Advises:

Neither you nor anybody ever said, "I want to be a cashier, server, cook, housekeeper or hourly worker when I grow up." Understand this so you can relate to your staff and they will believe you respect them for more than their work. Remember, their work here may not be offering them as much self-worth as being a manager offers us. It may not be offering the self-worth they feel about other aspects of their lives like parenting or their education. If you recognize these other aspects at work, you will increase their self-esteem at work.

Take the time to ask questions about your staff so you can find common things with which to relate to them. By finding a common passion such as a sport or music, you can then use these things as topics of conversation to open dialogue about performance or other issues. You may even be able to use examples from your common passion about how to be more successful at work. Perhaps this common passion requires a certain level of focus. A level of focus that, if brought into work, could greatly improve things.

As a dock supervisor, take pride in helping your staff find balance between what they need from the workplace and what their outside priorities are. If you do you will feel a tremendous amount of success for yourself, and your staff will be much more dedicated to you.

Have a friendly and direct one-on-one conversation with your employees and let them know you respect their priorities, but for four to six hours each shift, four or five days a week, they must respect the company's standards and work to achieve them. Cite examples of how doing so for this short amount of time will greatly reduce everyone's stress and make the workplace much more fun. Work can also be a temporary escape from the outside pressures employees have.

By outlining the expectations and standards in a conversation that includes their priorities, you will lay the groundwork for an environment that has fun with the standards. This means the workplace can be enjoyable while still focused on driving company standards. There is a sense of pride in working to achieve company objectives and a sense of accomplishment when achieved. For example, if a company has a customer payment transaction time of two minutes, talk about this objective before 'the rush' and have fun working to flow customers through the payment transaction during the rush. Afterwards create a sense of 'we won' by achieving the company's customer payment transaction time during a busy period. Make it a game.

Nobody ever said I want to be a waitress when I grow up.

Nobody ever said I want to be a house keeper when I grow up.

Nobody ever said I want to be a front desk clerk when I grow up.

Nobody ever said I want to be a call center worker when I grow up.

Respect them all.

Lesson Seven from Mr. Moss:

The Rules of the Game

Accepting the Business You Are In

Early in my Management career, I learned the rules of the game. I strongly believe that understanding these rules allowed me to focus on my performance and kept me moving forward in Management. I was running the restaurant and we had become Customer First Managers by getting our priorities in line with our customers'. A few months after we did this I started having some challenges with Brian that resulted in our owner, the engineer, coming in and assisting me with the situation.

Brian's performance had begun to slip. He wasn't getting his daily tasks one hundred percent complete as he had in the past and he seemed to be having mood swings that were affecting his performance. After a few incidents, I sat down with him.

"What is going on?" I asked.

"Everything's fine, why?"

"Well, you have seemed a bit moody lately, your schedules are getting done a little late and they have holes in them. And frankly, you are a little cranky at times. The reason I wanted to sit down with you now was to find out what I can do to get my old Brian back."

"So, I'm not allowed to make a mistake or two?" He was extremely defensive.

"Brian, come on. There is a real change in you and I am trying to find out what I can do to help get you back on track. I know nobody likes you in a bad mood less than you. When you are cranky, we have to tolerate you in small bursts, but you have to live with yourself all day. My sense is you are unhappy here."

He let out a long sigh, shook his head with a couple hard blinks and said, "I don't know."

I let him finish his thoughts.

"I … I just don't know. I've been killing myself, you know? I missed my Mom's birthday party a few weeks ago. There was a concert all my friends went to last Friday, but I obviously couldn't go because of this place and football season is starting soon but Sundays are a busy day for us so I'm sure to miss most of the games. I just … I don't know if this job is worth the sacrifice."

"Ok … well, Brian, I don't know what to tell you. This is what it is; weekends, nights, etcetera. It's the biz."

"I just don't think I can do it anymore. Don't know if I want to."

"Well, think about it and let me know."

A few days later Brian approached me and let me know he was going to be leaving. He had no plans and with an Associate's Degree in Management, his options were fairly limited. I told him I understood and called the owner to tell him about the situation. I would need to recruit and hire a new manager and the owner would want to meet the next manager and approve the hire.

"What can we do to save him?" asked the owner.

"I don't know. Like I told Brian, it is what it is, unless you want to close the restaurant a five p.m. and weekends, I don't see a solution."

There was a moment of silence and then the owner said, "Let me come in and have a meeting with both of you."

We all sat down a few days later. The owner asked Brian to tell him what was going on and Brian replayed the conversation he and I had.

"Brian, while my education is in Engineering and that's my primary business, I have been involved in and owned many businesses. All required a certain amount of sacrifice and dedication. I'll be the first to admit the restaurant business requires a bit more than others. But really, only a bit."

Brian was skeptical.

"Really, to be successful in anything, one thing that's part of the equation is to outwork your competition. Whether it's competition for a promotion or competing against another business, putting in the time is a big piece of the pie. So, what is it you are going to do when you leave us?"

"I haven't thought about it, really."

"You have a degree in Management, correct?"

Brian told him it was from the community college down the street.

"So management is your thing," the owner stated plainly.

"I guess."

"What would you like to do? I mean, what is your final career goal?" He asked Brian.

"Own my own business," Brian responded.

"Great. Do you think it will take sacrifice?"

"Of course."

"Entertain me a minute. Let's pretend you said 'become a doctor' instead of owning your own business as your career goal."

"Okay," Brian said with some question in his voice.

"Great. So you want to be a doctor. Any idea how many hours medical school requires of a person?

Not to mention you're paying for the sacrifice. Then, after four grueling years, you get to be an intern. 80 hour weeks, little pay, no respect from the 'real doctors,' it's brutal. Then you go work in another doctor's practice. Put in the hours for a few years, learn, cover his or her weekends and vacations, pay your dues, etc. It's a long time before you hang a sign saying 'Dr. Brian -New Patients Welcome.' Get it?"

"Not really."

"Patrick, anything you do worthwhile will require sacrifice. Period."

"Okay, but as you said, this business requires more sacrifice than others."

"A *bit* more. But if it was easy, everyone would do it."

"What does that mean for me?" Brian asked.

"It means you can create a career advantage for yourself by being willing to sacrifice."

"What if I'm not?"

"If you are not, then you will never own your own business or work your way to a senior Management role for any employer. But there is a solution. Something that will let you take control."

"What's that?"

"You must understand that any business you wish to be successful in will not give you a life outside of work."

"So what can I do, I don't really want to quit."

"*You have to carve a life out of it.*"

"What?"

"Carve a life out of it; careers don't give you a life. So you must take control and carve a life out of it."

Brian was interested and so was I, so he continued. The owner asked Brian when his mother's birthday was.

"June twelfth."

"Is it the twelfth every year?" asked the owner.

Brian laughed. "Of course."

"Did you ask for the day off?"

"No."

"Okay." The owner turned to me and said, "Can Brian have next June twelfth off?"

"Sure." I said.

"There you go. Dictate control of the situation. Carve a life out by planning ahead. Find out when your favorite band is playing ahead of time and give your employer ample notice. Make birthdays and other celebrations special by being involved in the planning and ensuring it works for you as well. It is very rare that you can't ask for a certain day off with enough notice to your boss. But you must take control because you accept that your work hours are a little different than others."

"What about the other things like dealing with our customers or the late hours or especially dealing with all the employees?"

"Brian, we are talking about the rules of the game now."

"What?"

"The rules of the game. When you chose Management as a career, you chose to accept the rules of the game. Just like a professional ball player can't complain or make excuses for the rules of his sport. He must perform within the rules and excel. But arguing with the referee or coaches or even the fans about the rules is not an option."

Brian was beginning to grasp the idea, but the owner needed to explain further.

"The rules of the game in Management are that you have long hours. Some businesses are a little longer than others, but Management and long hours are fairly synonymous these days. You also deal with the general public, which can be hard. You deal with hourly employees and turnover. You are responsible for others. In this business, like others, you must deal with vendors and availability of the product you sell. But accept these rules and move on. I once had a Manager in another business of mine who lived by the one percent rule."

"One percent rule?"

"Yes. He believed that one percent of all customers would be difficult. You know, the kind

of person who complains about everything and can't be pleased. In a business like this where you deal with hundreds of customers a week, there are bound to be some challenging people. Accept that and *expect* that as a rule of the game. Then, when you encounter a difficult customer, you will be much more relaxed in dealing with them. You also won't carry as much stress about those encounters because you know it's a rule of the game you play. You will do as you have done and work to please them, but manage by knowing the one percent rule and you will be happier. The reality is that these types of people are less than one percent, but we all know who they are and have to deal with them."

"That rule could apply to employees, too."

"Perhaps, Brian," said the owner. "That varies by labor market. But there are certainly many rules of the game when it comes to dealing with employees like managing turnover, back-to-school schedules, etcetera.

So Brian, I want you to think about where you would go from here. What would you say in your next interview? Would you say you know how to handle customers and manage employees? Would you say that you are willing to put in the hours? If that's the case, then carve a life out of it here. Accept the rules of the game here and let us keep you moving forward."

Brian agreed to think about it and left the table.

"Thank you," I said to the owner.

"My pleasure. You know, you need to take this advice, too. For yourself, and your people. Make sure you ask them if they have anything going on which they may need time off and help keep them relaxed about the rules of the game."

"I liked that part," I said. "Accepting those rules will reduce my stress. I am going to sit down with Brian and make a list of 'the rules' like we did for customer service points. We can then refer to the list when problems arise to help keep us in check. It will help us understand whether a problem is something we could foresee any way or not."

"Exactly," he said. "I fully expect a theft problem, employee relation problems, cost problems, vendor problems and more to come up within the next year. The key is to expect to deal with them, and quickly, because you can never expect the problems *not* to arise. Expecting to not have problems is foolish and a real false expectation. Moss, let me tell you that I understand you rarely create the problems you have to deal with, but you must understand that that's why you are here, to deal with those problems and work to foresee and prevent problems from occurring."

"Got it," I said, and carried those rules of the game forward from that point on in my career.

Mr. Moss Advises:

This lesson really helps managers understand their environment. I especially like to think of the rule regarding being busy. Most businesses are built with the expectation they will be busy. However, when they are busy, they then use the volume of business as an excuse for poor performance. Too often customers hear a worker say, "Sorry, we're really busy."

I always want to reply, "So you want to be slow?"

As a manager, *The Rules of the Game* are the first vital lesson you must learn in order to be successful. Just like a professional athlete, you must know the rules inside and out and work to perform and excel within them. Trying to change them is a waste of energy. Whether it is the hours of your industry, level of service your customers expect, type of employee your business hires, type of customer your business attracts or volume of business that must be dealt with on each shift, these are the rules of the game and Managers do not have the ability to change them.

By accepting *The Rules of the Game* you will remove a good portion of your own stress. When a problem arises, that is really just a rule of the game like an employee calling in sick, you can say to yourself, 'it's a rule of the game when dealing with employees, I better get someone in here to cover the shift.'

Today's business world makes very little time for family and self. Carve a life out for yourself by communicating your needs with your supervisor early and often. This lesson must apply to family and friends too. Communicate your job does not allow for much last minute flexibility and that you need their help in making future plans for events that are important to you. You have to carve a life out of it.

"What man's mind can create, man's character can control."

-Thomas Edison

About Mr. Moss

Mr. Moss is my fictional mentor. Moss stands for **M**anager **O**f **S**uperior **S**ervice and he is a combination of all the great people I have worked with over the last twenty years in customer service. These people have taught me many, many lessons. This book contains the seven lessons that I have found most vital in improving my career and improving the business I am Managing.

In recent years, I have referred to Mr. Moss more and more since 'leadership can be lonely' and I encourage all of you to create a fictional mentor who is a combination of all the very best skills from the very best people you have ever worked with.

About The Author

Robert "Bobby" Fitzgerald began working in customer service in 1984 at age 14. He studied Culinary Arts and Management at Johnson & Wales University, graduating in 1993. He became the youngest General Manager at Houston's Restaurants, Inc. by 1995. In 1999 he co-founded Cinzzetti's Restaurant Corp. which owns two restaurants under the Cinzzetti's brand, three under The White Chocolate Grill and its newest brand, Lincoln Whiskey Kitchen. He is involved in every aspect of the management of the business which has over 500 employees and locations in Chicago, Denver, Kansas City and Phoenix serving over 25,000 customers a week. Taking the lessons he has learned and taught to his managers into the classroom, he began speaking at Universities in 2002 on the subject of management and hospitality careers.

He lives in Scottsdale, Arizona with his wife, Shelley, and three children.

Special thanks to my wife Shelley who made this book possible by teaching me to carve a life out of it and constantly seek balance.

Lesson One Notes

_____

_____

_____

_____

_____

_____

_____

_____

_____

_____

_____

_____

_____

Lesson Two Notes

Lesson Three Notes

_____

_____

_____

_____

_____

_____

_____

_____

_____

_____

_____

_____

_____

Lesson Four Notes

Lesson Five Notes

Lesson Six Notes

_____

_____

_____

_____

_____

_____

_____

_____

_____

_____

_____

_____

_____

Lesson Seven Notes